P9-DMC-774

PROVERBS

SACRED TEACHINGS

Also Available

The Dhammapada: The Sayings of the Buddha
A Rendering by Thomas Byrom
with a preface by Ram Dass

PROVERBS

The Wisdom of Solomon

Translated and Introduced by

RABBI RAMI M. SHAPIRO

SACRED TEACHINGS

BELL TOWER NEW YORK

Published by Bell Tower, New York, New York.
Member of the Crown Publishing Group.

Random House, Inc. New York, Toronto, London, Sydney, Auckland
www.randomhouse.com

Bell Tower and colophon are registered trademarks of
Random House, Inc.

Printed in the United States of America

DESIGN BY BARBARA STURMAN

Library of Congress Cataloging-in-Publication Data

Bible. O.T. Proverbs. English. Shapiro. 2001.
    Proverbs : the wisdom of Solomon / translated and introduced
by Rami M. Shapiro.
        p. cm. — (Sacred teachings)
    I. Shapiro, Rami M. II. Title. III. Series.
    BS1463.S53 2001
    223'.705209—dc21   2001016549

ISBN 0-609-60889-4

10 9 8 7 6 5 4 3 2 1

First Edition

TO RICHARD J. FLANIGAN,
beloved father, friend, mentor, and guide

CONTENTS

THIS BOOK IS A collaboration stretching back thousands of years. Its contributors include King Solomon—the man traditionally thought to be the author and editor of these proverbs—generations of rabbinic sages and commentators, modern scholars both Jewish and Christian, and my editor at Bell Tower, Toinette Lippe. Of them all, I think the king and Toinette have had the most influence.

King Solomon may or may not have had anything to do with the original compilation of these ancient words of wisdom. Since he was thought to be the wisest human being who ever lived, it is not difficult to see why authorship was ascribed to him. Who else was capable of it?

I am not interested in the historicity of Solomon's authorship. Proving or disproving his role neither adds to nor detracts from the power of these sayings. Yet as I read, reread, and ultimately freely translated these teachings, I could not help but imagine Solomon sharing them with his people. It was his voice I heard in my head as I read. It was his counsel that suggested new ways to understand the text, ways that revived their relevance for our time and indeed for any time. So I am indebted to him for his patience with me.

I have a similar indebtedness to Toinette Lippe. Toinette may not be Solomon, but she is British and that is almost as good. Her grasp of English challenged my choice of words on almost every line. She has an uncanny ability to know what I am trying to say and then help me say it with more clarity, grace, and power. Where Solomon set the arrows of Proverbs into the quiver of history, Toinette sharpened their tips to deepen their impact on the present.

As with my other books of free translation, this one is best read in tandem with a more traditional translation. I suggest this for two reasons: first, to insure the integrity of the text itself; second, to highlight its message. I seek not simply to translate a word but to recover its meaning, and in so doing I often depart significantly from the conventional reading. By comparing my understanding of the original Hebrew with that of others, you can begin to uncover additional meanings for yourself. More literal translations of Proverbs often result in a moralistic diatribe that is quite off-putting. This could not be farther from the original intention. Proverbs is a collection of timeless insights into perennial issues, as I hope my version makes clear.

KING DAVID WAS DEAD. The young Prince Solomon ben David had taken his place on the throne of Israel. Solomon had no leadership experience, and although he may have watched his father with great intensity, he himself was now king, and the pressure was enormous. One night he slept, and God appeared to him in a dream. Ask for one gift, God said, and it will yours. The dream king responded:

> You showed great kindness to Your servant, David, my father, because he walked before You with truth and justice and with an upright heart; and You were also generous enough to give him a son who sits on his throne this very day. And now, Adonai, my God, You have crowned Your servant in place of David,

my father. Yet I am young and inexperienced, and
do not know how to conduct myself as a man, let
alone a leader. Your servant is in the midst of Your
people whom You have chosen, a large nation that
cannot be counted because of its abundance. Grant
Your servant an understanding heart so that I am
able to judge Your people, to discriminate between
good and evil; for who can judge this formidable
people of Yours? (1 Kings 3:6–9)

God was pleased with Solomon's request
because he did not ask for anything for himself,
and He granted it.

Behold I have given you a wise and understanding heart: there has never been anyone like you
before, nor will anyone like you ever arise again.
(1 Kings 3:12)

What would you ask for if God offered to
fulfill your deepest desire? Power? Wealth? Sex?
Happiness? Health? Solomon asked for wisdom.
When the young king awoke, the deepest truths

of life and how best to live them were clear to him, and to his credit, he shared them freely.

Solomon's first book was *Shir haShirim,* the Song of Songs, a passionate tribute to sensuality and erotic love. His final book was *Koheleth,* Ecclesiastes, a meditation on mortality and what really matters in life. In between writing these books he wrote aphorisms and collected the folk wisdom of his time—the short pithy teachings that are often the spice of human speech. This collection is called *Mishlei,* Proverbs.

There are three major themes to Proverbs: overcoming ignorance, practicing self-discipline, and having personal integrity.

Solomon divides people into two categories: the wise and the ignorant. There is, most likely, much mingling of these in each of us, but for Solomon the distinction between them is clear and absolute:

10:5

The wise learn from the softest whisper;
the ignorant sleep through the loudest alarm.

10:23

The ignorant laugh at evil;
the wise laugh at themselves.

The ignorant justify their folly;

the wise seek the counsel of the just.

On first reading I found this kind of teaching simplistic. Solomon eliminates the grays of life in favor of a black-and-white dualism that makes morality and right action appear self-righteous and prudish. The more I worked with Proverbs, however, and the more I sought to apply them to my own life, the more I realized that much of what I took for legitimate gray was in fact clearly black and white. I preferred to think in terms of gray to rationalize away questionable actions, or to confuse things so that I could avoid doing the right thing.

The fact is, life is fairly simple. There is birth and death; good and evil; right and wrong; justice and injustice; honesty and dishonesty. We complicate life by refusing to respond to reality as it is. Most of the time it is not difficult to identify the right path. What is difficult is actually walking it.

Not long ago, on a flight from Miami to Chicago, I struck up a conversation with the man sitting next to me, a financial analyst named Jason. When he found out I was a rabbi, he paused for a long moment and said: "I'm dying. I have a rare form of cancer, and there is nothing anyone can do for me. I'm forty-six years old. I have a wife and three kids. The oldest is only nine. How the hell does this happen to people? And why the hell is it happening to me?

"My closest friend says I have to experience this cancer in order to work out some error in a past life. My priest says it's God's will. What kind of God wills this?"

Jason seemed a bit out of breath. I invited him to keep talking, but he had nothing more to say. It was my turn.

"Listen, Jason, I can't pretend to know what you're going through. I have no solution to offer, nor anything to make sense out of your cancer. I can give you my opinion on some of the issues you raised, but that's about it."

Jason nodded, and I continued.

"There is no reason why this is happening to you. Your friend is full of crap. And saying this is

God's will is simply another way of saying shit happens. It does, and you are living proof. I believe in reality, and the reality is that you are a young man with a wife and three small children, and you are dying. Asking *Why me?* is a distraction from that reality. There is no final answer to *Why me?* You can invent possibilities right up until the moment you die, and none of them will really satisfy you.

"Jason, I'm not trying to be harsh, just clear. You are going to hear a lot of garbage about why this is happening to you. Most of it is offered in order to comfort the person offering it. The only comfort you can find in your situation is to respond to it with the best that is in you."

"What does that mean?"

"You have to do what you can to maintain your health for as long as possible. You have to do what you can to see to the financial security of your family. And you have to do what you can to show your kids the right way to die."

"The right way to die?"

"Show them that death is sad, maybe even

tragic, but that people can handle the sad and the tragic in a loving way. Love them so much that you are willing to share your feelings with them. Love them so much that you are willing to spend as much time with them as they need. Love them so much that you do not close the door of your heart to them when you are most lost and they are the most frightened."

"The only thing I'm sure of is that I'm dying, and that I love my wife and kids."

"That's reality. Now respond to it."

"Just die and love?"

"The other way around," I said. "Just love and die."

When I share this story with people, they often criticize me for being unduly harsh and cold. You may feel the same way. The fact is that I had only a few minutes to get to the heart of a very serious matter. I could have complicated things sufficiently to pass the time on the airplane and leave Jason with a lot of theoretical ideas to ponder. But that would have been a cop-out. Life isn't that compli-cated. His situation was extremely simple: love and die. Maybe the same could be said of all of us.

The Book of Proverbs addresses us as if we were all Jasons in need of clarity and truth. No theories. No excuses. Just love and die. It is their ability to cut to the heart of the matter that gives Solomon's proverbs their power. They don't deal in grays.

For Solomon there are two states of mind: disciplined and slothful. The disciplined mind focuses on the task at hand and does it as best it can. The slothful mind looks for excuses for inaction, or seeks to cut corners through violence, dishonesty, and theft.

Solomon calls us "ignorant," "lazy," and "foolish" when we complicate the simple, and substitute the easy for the good. He calls us "wise" when we cease to hide from reality and openly and honestly face the truth of each moment.

Is Solomon wrong to approach life so simply? Are his proverbs any less useful for their being so stark? On the contrary. It is Solomon's honest portrayal of reality and his clear prescriptions for how to live it that give the book its power and timelessness.

To benefit from reading Solomon's proverbs, you have to have the courage to see the world as he does: simply, and without the smoke and mirrors of our rationalizations and excuses. Proverbs forces us to examine our lives and how we are living them without the benefit of psychological sophistry and New Age babble. We are either disciplined or lazy. We are either doing good or doing bad. We are either curbing our desires or succumbing to them. We are either wise or ignorant. We are either a student of wisdom or a puppet of desire.

Facing this reality is a challenge. Your mind will find excuses to discount almost every teaching. You need to be patient with yourself, but not yielding. Here is how I suggest you read this book.

Proverbs is meant to be savored. Read it slowly. Keep it on your nightstand and read a little each night before going to sleep. Or write down one or two sayings on a note card and think about them during the day. Use them for contemplation or as the opening sentence in your diary or journal.

Whatever you do with these teachings, don't dismiss them as simplistic. They are simple, yes, but

not simplistic. If you allow them to speak to you
honestly; if you do not defend yourself against
their meaning and their implication for your life;
if you listen carefully to the ancient king's instructions, you will change for the better and grow
in wisdom.

R.M.S.

The Nine Foundational Teachings

INTRODUCTION

1:1–7

These are the proverbs and parables of Solomon,
    son of David, King of Israel:
A guide to insight, understanding, and spiritual
    discipline
to help you become generous, honest, and balanced.
They are offered to the simple that they may gain
    knowledge;
to the young that they may find direction;
to the learned that they may peer behind the
    words and attain wisdom;
for I speak in metaphors both simple and
    profound,
wise words that hide deeper meanings.

Begin with this: The foundation of wisdom is the
    selfless awe of God.

Skeptics deny that this is so, and the ignorant
   ignore the discipline that leads to it,
but you need not be among them.

THE FIRST TEACHING

1:8–19

You are guided from the very beginning:
the instruction of your father—do not abandon it!
the teaching of your mother—do not forsake it!
Let their discipline adorn you as a necklace and
    crown,
so that you do not fall victim to foolish desires,
who, like thieves, lay an ambush for the innocent.
They call to you: *Come, join us. We will murder*
    the weak
and fill our homes with their wealth and dignity;
there will be a single pouch for us all.
Do not set your feet on their path, for it leads
    only to self-destruction.
They rush to violence, driven by a jealous hunger,
    never satisfied.
When you go forth to trap a bird, what do you do?

You spread grain to lure it in.

The bird takes the grain, you take the bird.

When evil seeks to entrap you, it does the same.

Desire takes the place of grain, and you are no
    smarter than the bird.

The trap looks so innocent, yet its jaws crush both
    body and soul.

1:20–33

How different it is with wisdom!

She lays no snares and has no need to hide.

She sings openly in the street;

she speaks clearly,

her voice rising above the tumult of the market
    and the gates of the city.

It is one thing if a child surrenders to desire,

but when adults act childishly, it is true folly.

You will never outgrow cynicism and foolishness.

You are never too old for wickedness.

You can resist wisdom's words all your life,

yet she will never give up on you.

Wisdom speaks deep within you saying:

I will continue to share my spirit with you.

I will speak my truth, though you refuse to hear me.
I will stretch forth my hand though you slap it away.
I will offer counsel though you plug your ears.
I will not laugh, knowing that all your dramas are born
  of ignorance.
I will remain compassionate though you continue to
  choose trouble over truth.

Yet even I have limits
and I worry that I will tire and withdraw.
Then when fearsome darkness swallows you
and misfortune overtakes you;
when your body fails you and your spirit flags;
when at last you call out: Wisdom, please reveal
  yourself to me!
I will be too weak to respond.
When you finally come in search of Me, I may be too lost
  to be found.

If you hate knowledge and spurn wisdom,
if you reject my counsel and refuse my direction,
all you have left is the bitter fruit of your own orchards,
the emptiness of your own schemes.

30 *Your own recklessness will kill you, a homicide at the*
        hand of desire.
Listen to me, and my words will protect you;
heed me, and you can face your strongest desires with
        tranquillity.

THE SECOND TEACHING

2:1–8

Will you heed my words and accept my direction?

Then open your ears to wisdom and incline your
heart to clarity.

Call on understanding, a trusted mother whose
love is all you need.

Seek her joyfully as though she were a hidden
treasure.

Only joy reveals the grandeur and grace of God.

God is unbounded wisdom, knowledge, and
insight.

Wisdom upon wisdom, God is the foundation
of truth.

Only the attentive will find God, only the simple
will know truth;

and God will grant these to you, safeguarding the
    paths of justice
and protecting those who choose to walk them.

2:9–13

When wisdom is embraced, righteousness, justice,
    and fairness are known;
all paths are illumined and you need fear no
    detour.
When wisdom enters your heart and knowledge
    your soul,
you will perceive the order of the universe and
    never despair.
You will be rescued from your own dark
    inclinations,
and not even the cleverest lies will fool you.

2:14–22

You can, of course, forsake the upright path and
    wander in the dark.
You can take pleasure in evil and rejoice in
    clouding the mind with words.
You can choose the crooked road or one with
    no way out.
And still wisdom will rescue you.

You can abandon my teaching and pursue desire.
You can banish insight from your home
and open your doors to those who cannot face
   the truth.
But as long as you choose this road, the living
   path is lost.
Choose differently: seek wisdom and walk the
   good path.
The upright dwell in timeless wisdom; the whole-
   hearted can never be lost,
but the wicked are driven from every place
and the faithless have nowhere to call home.

THE THIRD TEACHING

3:1–4

Remember my teaching
and observe my precepts.
My words will bless your years with tranquillity
and peace.
Let kindness and truth adorn you, speak of them
often,
and inscribe them on the tablets of your heart that
they shape your every thought.
Do this, and you are beloved in realms both
human and divine.

3:5–12

Do not make a crutch of ego; lean on God alone.
Adhere to the good, and your path will be smooth.
Do not imagine that you are wise.
Know only that you do not know.
Stand in awe of the Infinite, and turn away from evil.

In this way you strengthen both body and soul.

Know from Whom success comes, and give
generously to those in need.

Your wealth will increase as a result of your
generosity;

none can fathom the rewards of those who share
their wealth.

Not everything that happens will be enjoyable,

and not every word you hear will be kind,

yet receive everything as a gift and a teaching.

3:13–26

Only men and women of wisdom and
understanding are worthy of praise.

They deal in something more valuable than silver
or gold.

For wisdom is more precious than pearls,

and desire for anything else is empty.

She is the way to everlasting life, true wealth,
and honor.

Her way is pleasant, and all her paths are peace.

She is a Tree of Life to those who embrace her,

and those that cleave to her find happiness.

Wisdom is the foundation of the earth,

THE NINE FOUNDATIONAL TEACHINGS

and understanding the pillar of sky.
A divine order patterns all of creation,
from the timeless ocean to the fleeting dew.
Keep your attention on wisdom,
and do not allow yourself to be distracted.
Watch the patterns of creation.
This will enliven your soul and bring you grace
    and tranquillity.
Seeing truth, you can walk forward in confidence
without stumbling out of ignorance.
When you sleep, you will not be afraid;
your sleep will come easily.
When you wake, you will not be anxious
nor worry about your fate,
for you rest safely in the divine
and your feet do not stray from the path.

3:27–35

Do not hold back from helping others;
share what you have without reservation.
Do not say to the needy: *Ask me again tomorrow,*
when you can do something today.
Do not sow seeds of evil nor betray those who
    trust you.

Do not quarrel even with those that do not have
  your best interests at heart.
Do not envy the violent nor imitate them,
for one who strays from the path of peace turns
  away from all that is holy;
only the upright are intimate with God.
The houses of the wicked are condemned, but the
  homes of the just are blessed.
Do not underestimate the power of association:
align yourself with scoffers, and you will scoff;
practice humility, and you will be appreciated.
The wise inherit honor, the legacy of the fool
  is disgrace.

THE FOURTH TEACHING

4:1–6

Listen and attend, and understanding will follow.

You have been given a good teaching; do not
abandon it.

Do not imagine that what I say is mere opinion.

I had a father and a mother whom I loved.

My father taught me: *Let my words sustain your heart;*
practice my discipline and live.

Do whatever it takes to acquire wisdom and understanding.

My mother taught me: *But do not imagine that words*
are a substitute for action;

no matter how wise you are, you must act justly and
with compassion.

Do not forsake this teaching; it will protect you.

Love it, and it will keep you from harm.

What is the beginning of wisdom? Wisdom itself.

There is no process, no technique, no moving
   toward.

She resides in every encounter.

Recognize her, and find peace.

Embrace her, and find honor.

Then your words will be accepted and heeded.

I teach you because I love you;

may you live a long and peaceful life.

I have instructed you in wisdom and set before
   you the way of tranquillity.

When you walk, walk freely, secure in the
   knowledge that you will not stray.

When you run, run effortlessly, knowing that your
   foot will not stumble.

Be diligent in your practice, and do not abandon it.

Keep it dear to you, for it is life itself.

Do not nurse doubts and schemes;

they may come to visit you, but you need not
   invite them in.

Reject the temptation to do evil, and do not
daydream of taking revenge.

How can you free yourself from the clutches of
evil desire?
Refrain from acting on your desires;
do not give in to them, not even occasionally.
Avoid situations that arouse such unwanted desire.
Do not seek to uproot desire, but steer around it.
Habits are powerful and rob you of your sleep;
they are so contagious, you may cause others to
falter as well.
Such habits do violence to your soul and steal your
dignity.
Like the dawn that grows to noonday brightness,
so the path of wisdom begins in shadow and
grows in brilliance.
But the path of the wicked is dark, and their every
step uncertain.

4:20–27

Be attentive to both the surface and what is below.
Do not accept a thing on first hearing, but
examine it carefully.

Set wisdom as a lens before your eye that your
    vision be clear.
Turn your heart to her that your intention is good.
For wisdom is life, and one who finds her finds
    inner health.
Protect your heart above all else,
for the heart determines the quality of your life.

How to protect the heart?
Do not gossip or deceive another with your words.
Close your eyes to the imperfections of others.
Consider the likely consequences of your actions,
    and align them with the good.
When the good is known, do it without hesitation.
Do not waver to the right nor to the left;
and do not place your foot on the path of evil.

THE FIFTH TEACHING

Attend now to my words;
incline your ear to grasp my meaning.
Express your thoughts with wisdom and your
   words with truth.
Yet even then the sweet honey of desire will
   tempt you.
Slippery as oil is the way of desire.
Taste this honey and your lips swell with bitterness;
follow this path and a double-edged desire will
   cleave you in two.
The way of desire leads only to the grave; the path
   itself is death.

Make no comparison between these two paths,
   for that legitimizes them both.

Do not imagine that they offer you a choice, for
    that sets you at a crossroad.
The wise do not ask which is the true path; their
    feet are naturally drawn to it.

5:7–12

So avoid comparison and the illusion of choice.
Abide in your heart, for without this connection
    each year is more bitter than the next.
Succumb to desire, and all your treasure will
    be lost;
your body will be exhausted from worry,
your soul consumed by doubt, and your heart
    become brittle as glass.
Your final days will be plagued with self-criticism
and your last moments haunted by regret.
Your final thoughts will be cries of despair:
*How could I have hated discipline, and turned a deaf
    ear to my teachers?*
*How could I have ignored wisdom's promise and
    surrendered to fleeting pleasure?*

5:13–19

Yet do not put your trust in teachers alone.
Drink their deep store of wisdom,

but seek out also water from your own well.
Do this, and the thirsty will come to you saying:
Our souls are parched, our hearts like baked leather;
give us a sip of your water to help us revive.

This wisdom is yours alone, unclouded by others'
    words and schemes.
The source of your wisdom is blessedness.
Drink it, and experience the joy of a lover's
    first kiss.

As mountain goats run to each other, so will
    others run to you.
You will nurse them with the milk of wisdom,
and both of you will be drunk on love.

5:20–23

Be not seduced by desire.
She promises passion, but her breast is dry.
Align your deeds with godliness,
for your actions alone determine your fate—
sin leads only to sin;
despair brings only despair;
the sands of delusion will swirl around you,

and you will be blind to truth;
you will die, and what wisdom you had will
    evaporate in the hot wind.

THE SIXTH TEACHING

6:1–5

Remember what promises you make.

Do not pledge to one

and then make a conflicting promise to another.

In this way your mouth becomes a snare and your
words trap you.

If this occurs, go to the first and humble yourself.

Do not rest or sleep until you have done what you
can to set the matter right.

6:6–11

Do you need a model for your actions? Look to
the ant!

Adopt her way of life and grow wise.

No one gives her instructions,

yet she prepares her food in summer and gathers
her grain at harvest time.

She takes care of her own needs and does not steal
   from others.

Do not be lazy about the work of wisdom,
hiding in your bed, asleep to the knowledge that
   is your birthright.
The dawn comes and you groan:
Just a bit more sleep, a few more minutes;
let me tuck my hand under my head
and close my eyes for a little while longer.
And what happens while you dawdle?
Poverty of spirit overtakes you,
and sloth blocks your way like a shield.

6:12–15

Without self-discipline you are enslaved to desire,
and every word you utter promotes a scheme.
You wink at the truth and cause others to doubt.
You feign humility as a ploy to spread evil gossip.
You point a finger of blame and sully the
   reputation of the blameless.
Your innermost thoughts are corrupt;
your mind says *yes* when your heart pleads *no.*

Your every desire is for exploitation.
You delight in setting friends at odds.
So intent on bringing misfortune to others,
your own situation goes unnoticed
and evil catches you unaware.
It deals you a fatal blow.

6:16–19

Six things cut you off from the holy,
a seventh makes even your soul a monster:
an arrogant manner, a deceitful tongue, murderous
    thoughts,
a thieving heart, feet eager to run after evil, a
    scheming mind,
and a tendency to arouse violence in those who
    once lived in peace.

6:20–22

Do not forget the rules of justice
or the subtle teachings of compassion.
Bind your heart with them,
and tie them as a scarf around your neck
that whatever comes out of your mouth is
    tempered by goodness.
Do this, and they will guide your steps;

your sleep will be dreamless, your waking free
    from guilt;
and wisdom will speak with you like a close friend.

6:23–26

Deeds are lamps, and wisdom the flame that
    lights them.
Learn from your mistakes; there is no shame in error.
Close your mouth to gossip and your ear to
    falsehood.
How lovely is desire; do not be tempted by it.
How attractive its promise; do not be seduced by
    its charms.
For desire will steal your wisdom
and force you to beg for a slice of bread when
    whole loaves are your due.
Your life is precious; do not sacrifice it to evil.

6:27–35

Even the fire walker's feet are sometimes scorched
    by hot coals.
How can your heart not burn when walking the
    path of desire?
There is desire in all of us, and none can escape it;
you may not root it out, but you can rein it in.

If you are caught stealing because you are hungry,
the judge will understand: pay what you owe
    and depart.
But there is no mercy for those who deliberately
    inflame the heart.
Their souls are crushed, they are humiliated,
and their disgrace is never-ending.
The flame of truth engulfs them,
and no one pities them.
There is no ransoming of the wicked,
and justice is not thwarted by bribes.

THE SEVENTH TEACHING

Listen to me, and treasure my instruction.

My words are the key to life; without them all
  you have is existence.

Just as you shield your eyes from the sun so as
  not to be blinded,

these words will shield your heart from desire
  and protect your wisdom.

Tie them like a string on your finger to remind
  you of righteousness.

Align your heart with mercy, and your head
  with justice,

so that your hand does what is right.

Call wisdom your sister, and understanding
  your niece,

for the latter is born of the former.

Stay close to them, and neither envy nor lust will
    distract you from the good.

7:6–8

I have looked through the lattice of the heart
and seen the ways of undisciplined desire.
The simple and the young are easy prey, for they
    lack self-control.
Yet do not imagine that they are innocent,
for evil cannot enter without our consent.
Even young people must approach the threshold
    of desire
before evil can push them through the door.

7:9–20

Without wisdom you walk in perpetual twilight,
seeing only shadows and understanding little.
You are prey to evil desires.
Seductively dressed, they brazenly call you,
and your heartbeat quickens with anticipation;
crazy sexual images race through your mind.
Loud and demanding, they hound you.
You recognize them in the dark corners of
    your heart.

You feel their kisses on your mouth, and you
  tremble with desire.

They thrust their faces up against your own and
  whisper:

*Do not think us evil; we come simply to make peace, to
  lead you toward the good.*

*That is why we have arrived. That is why we are offering
  you this chance.*

*And besides, how could we have found you unless God
  wanted us to?*

Why should you give up the pleasures of the world?

They draw you into bed, cover you in the softest
  Egyptian linen;

your head spins from their perfume—myrrh, aloes,
  and cinnamon.

They call to you sweetly:

Come, enjoy yourself until the grave beckons.

If you must repent, do it then.

Do you still think God cares about you and your world?

*Look how the evil prosper! They find joy in every desire.
  Why don't you?*

*The righteous God kills mercilessly; why would you
  choose to be a victim?*

Your wisdom is overturned;

your understanding is lost;

and the fear of sin is drowned out by desire.

Wisdom is lost no matter how frantically you
seek her.

And you succumb, saying: *I will make amends if
she returns.*

7:21–23

You cannot withstand such seduction;

temptation's logic is inexorable.

It will lead you as an ox to the slaughter;

your own thoughts lead you on; there is no one
else to blame.

Like a poisonous snake striking the heel of the
careless,

like a sheep trotting mindlessly into the snare,

you will stumble after desire until remorse splits
your liver like an arrow.

7:24–25

Is there no defense against desire?

Listen to me, and heed the words of my mouth:

Let wisdom reign in your heart,

and do not race after every emotion.

Do not assume that pleasure is the same as
    goodness,
or that feelings are a guide to righteousness.
Desire has slain many mightier than you.
The way of undisciplined desire leads only to
    the grave;
the chambers of death are full of those who
    lacked the strength to be wise.

THE EIGHTH TEACHING

Do not think that wisdom is silent in the face
   of desire.
She calls out boldly, her voicing rising above
   the din.
There is nowhere she fears to go.
Atop distant mountains,
on crowded highways,
at the crossroads of decision,
she stands ready to guide you.
By the city gates,
even at the doorway of destruction she cries out
   to you:
Listen to me!
If you are too simple to discern wisdom,
at least let me teach you how to avoid evil.
If you are wise enough to know better

yet weak enough to succumb to desire,
at least let me show you how to use your discretion,
to exercise control over random passions.

8:6–9

Wisdom says:
Listen and my words will uplift you;
my mouth will utter honest words.
I will speak only truth to you,
for wickedness is poison to my lips.
I will speak of righteousness without twisted logic or
     perverted reasons.
One who understands will recognize the purity of
     my words
and the integrity of my teaching.

8:10–11

Choose inner discipline over silver,
and knowledge over the finest gold.
My way is superior to pearls, and is more valuable
     than anything else.

8:12–17

I am wisdom;
I dwell in watchfulness;
I provide insight into the way of life.

The godly reject evil.
I reject even the paths to evil:
the paths of pride, arrogance, and a lying tongue.
My words are counsel and guide;
I am understanding, and in me is strength.
Through me flows all justice and righteousness;
from me comes discernment and leadership.
I love those who love me
and reveal myself fully to those who search me out.

8:18–20

Integrity and honor are my wealth,
and great good fortune lies with me.
My fruit is more precious than the finest gold;
it is superior to the choicest silver.
If you take up the path of compassion,
I will lead you along the road of justice.

8:21–31

I fill the hearts of those who love me;
they will never lack for insight.
I am the deep grain of creation, the subtle current of life.
God fashioned me before all things;
I am the blueprint of creation.

I was there from the beginning, from before there was
    a beginning.
I am independent of time and space, earth and sky.
I was before depth was conceived,
before springs bubbled with water,
before the shaping of mountains and hills,
before God fashioned the earth and its bounty,
before the first dust settled on the land.

When God prepared the heavens, I was there.
When the circle of the earth was etched into the face of
    the deep, I was there.
When the stars and planets soared into their orbit,
when the deepest oceans found their level
and the dry land established the shores,
I was there.
I stood beside God as firstborn and friend.
My nature is joy, and I gave God constant delight.
Now that the world is inhabited, I rejoice in it.
I will be your true delight if you will heed my teachings.

8:32–36

So listen to me:
Follow me and be happy.

Practice my discipline and grow wise.
Abandon cynicism and doubt.
I bring joy to those who listen;
I bring happiness to those who attend me.
Like watchmen at their post, they do not stray.
They see the play of wisdom.
Find me, and find life.
Find me, and find grace.
Turn your back on me, and choose death.

THE NINTH TEACHING

9:1–6

Wisdom's house is built with many pillars.
It is magnificent and easy to find.
Inside she has cooked a fine meal and sweetened
    her water with wine.
Her table is set.
She sends maidens to the tallest towers to
    summon you.
To the simple they call:
Come, enter here.
To those who lack understanding they say:
Come, eat my food, drink my wine.
Abandon your empty life, and walk in the way
    of understanding.

9:7–9

Wrestling with desire
fans its embers into flame.

Besides, your arguments are met with scorn,
and your energy could be put to better use.
Rebuking desire makes it the center of attention.
Turn your attention to wisdom, and let desire cool
    from neglect.
Wisdom thrives on discipline; truth flourishes
    when errors are corrected.

9:10–12

Those who walk with wisdom walk in wonder.
Marvel at the miracle of life, and gain
    understanding.
Stand in awe of the mystery, and enter the eternal
    present.
Become wise, and you understand who you are:
you know what moves you, and you act almost
    without effort.
If you scorn this path, your heart is diminished,
your mind clouded, and you carry a heavy burden.
Everything you do goes awry.

9:13–18

Wisdom is not the only voice you will hear.
Foolishness too has her house and her servants.

She sits at the doorway of her house and flaunts
    ignorance as if it were gold.
Her servants also climb the city's towers and
    call out to you.
To the simple they say: *Turn in here.*
To those whose hearts are dry they say:
You think wisdom's wine is sweet?
My stolen water is even sweeter.
You think wisdom's feast is filling?
Eat my bread in secret and your mouth will taste
    pure pleasure.
Do you know she sleeps with corpses?
Do you know her house is the gateway to
    the grave?

The First Collection of Shorter Sayings

10:1

These are the proverbs of Solomon:

Be wise and increase the joy of heaven;
Be foolish and increase the suffering of earth.

10:2

Death cannot be bribed,
but generosity outlasts the grave.

10:3

In famine wisdom fills the belly,
while sin brings starvation even in the midst
    of plenty.

10:4

Tip the balance by lying, and your life is
    impoverished;
uphold honesty, and the result is prosperity.

10:5

The wise learn from the softest whisper;
the ignorant sleep through the loudest alarm.

10:6

The good reap blessings;
the wicked chew on violence.

10:7

Seek out the righteous, and blessings will follow;
yearning for the wicked brings ruin.

10:8

The wise heart listens to others;
a foolish tongue wears out its audience.

10:9

Walk in innocence, and you are safe from harm;
walk in deceit, and your every step is revealed.

10:10

Inner confusion leads to sadness;
pretending to be what you are not mars each hour
    with worry.

10:11

Straight talk is a wellspring of life;
deception is a mask for violence.

10:12

Anger sharpens every conflict;
love binds every wound.

10:13

Innocent mistakes are soon corrected;
deliberate evil invites a blow on the back.

10:14

The words of the wise are few;
the babbling of fools leads to ruin.

10:15

Wisdom protects wealth;
ignorance induces only poverty.

10:16

Wise deeds bring life;
wickedness hastens death.

10:17

The disciplined live;
the lazy are lost.

10:18

No words, however pleasant, conceal the seething
    of an angry heart;
one who gives voice to every hurt is a fool.

10:19

The more you talk, the more you risk offense;
the wise purse their lips in silence.

10:20

The words of the wise are precious;
the heart of the wicked is shriveled.

10:21

Wise words nourish many;
the ignorant starve for lack of understanding.

10:22

Wisdom alone brings riches;
worrying never improves a situation.

10:23

The ignorant laugh at evil;
the wise laugh at themselves.

10:24

What you fear, you will find;
the wise desire only wisdom.

10:25

Wickedness is devastated by the storm,
but wisdom is the foundation of the world.

Vinegar sets your teeth on edge,
smoke stings your eyes,
and half-hearted effort is doomed to failure.

Wonder enhances life;
worry shortens it.

The righteous anticipate only gladness;
the hope of the wicked is tainted by fear.

The path of God strengthens the innocent;
those who build with iniquity raise only ruins.

The righteous never stumble;
the wicked are never tranquil.

The words of the wise ripen on the vine;
the yapping of fools shrivels on the ground.

One whose judgment is honest,
whose scales are balanced, this one is blessed;
but the deceitful pervert the way of God.

11:2

Arrogance is its own disgrace;
modesty its own reward.

11:3

The just are guided by simplicity;
the wicked seed corruption with complication.

11:4

No matter how wealthy the wicked, anger destroys
them.
The generosity of the just saves them from danger.

11:5

Justice smooths a pitted path,
but the wicked stumble over their own evil.

11:6

The wise are rescued by justice,
but the wicked are trapped by their own lies.

11:7

When the wicked die, their schemes die with them,
and the hope of their accomplishments is
shattered.

11:8

There is evil in this world, and the wicked attract
it like a magnet.

The just are wise enough to not be ensnared.

11:9

The wicked speak in order to harm.
The wise use words to heal.

11:10

People rejoice when the good are rewarded;
They also rejoice at the misfortune of the wicked.

11:11

The prosperity of the just is shared by the
     community;
the wicked sow discord and rob the people
     of blessing.

11:12

The empty-hearted are quick to criticize;
a heart filled with understanding values silence.

11:13

The wicked are a font of gossip;
the faithful protect every confidence.

11:14

You cannot control your nature alone;
salvation lies in listening to the wise.

11:15

The wicked default on their loans;
the wise honor their commitments.

11:16

Honor is retained through graciousness;
power is maintained through intimidation.

11:17

Those that are kind are well treated by others;
the cruel are a plague upon themselves.

11:18

The wicked choke on their greed;
the generous find happiness in the act of giving.

11:19

The selfless inherit life;
the reward of the self-centered is death.

11:20

A selfish heart cannot find God;
an open heart cannot lose Him.

11:21

Evil influence reaches no farther than the wicked's
    arm;
good deeds are a raft for generations.

A golden ring cannot hide a pig's snout,
nor a beautiful face disguise an evil heart.

The righteous trust in goodness;
the wicked place their hope in anger.

The generous are not anxious about wealth;
the stingy always fear poverty.

Share in another's joy, and your own joy is
    kindled.
Fill the bellies of the hungry, and your own
    stomach is filled.

One who hoards is cursed;
one who shares is blessed.

Seek the happiness of others, and you will
    find God;
seek their destruction, and you will fall into
    your own snare.

11:28

Trust in your own power and fail;
know your limitations and flourish.

11:29

Be of two minds, and your legacy is the wind;
bond with the wise, and enjoy prosperity.

11:30

Righteousness sows the seeds of life;
wisdom redeems the souls of the lost.

11:31

The good see goodness all around them;
the wicked are rewarded with their own malice.

12:1

Love knowledge, and you will value discipline;
only the stupid are deaf to criticism.

12:2

A good person is a conduit for the truth,
and a schemer a sluice for evil.

12:3

Wickedness is built on a weak foundation,
but righteousness can withstand any disaster.

A faithful spouse can save a faltering marriage;
an unfaithful one hastens its demise.

The mind of the wise is uncluttered and empty;
the mind of the wicked is crowded with schemes.

Even the pleasant words of the wicked intend
    violence,
while the misstatements of the wise come from a
    loving heart.

The wicked die and leave a legacy of wind.
The righteous die and leave a legacy of life.

Wisdom draws praise,
a twisted heart only shame.

The simple are satisfied, serving themselves,
while the pompous starve waiting to be fed.

The humane care for their animals;
the thoughtless neglect them.

12:11

Till the soil of your character and reap goodness;
the pursuit of pleasure leads the heart astray.

12:12

The wicked are driven by jealousy; in the end
    they have nothing.
The root of the wise is grounded in integrity.

12:13

Guard your tongue and have no fear;
honesty frees you from worry.

12:14

Right speech is wise speech;
right action brings its own reward.

12:15

The ignorant justify their folly;
the wise seek the counsel of the just.

12:16

The ignorant react with anger;
the wise watch their emotions come and go.

12:17

Make truth a habit, and your words will be trusted.
Bear false witness, and you become the epitome
    of deceit.

The tongue of the wicked cuts like a sharp sword;
the words of the wise bring healing.

Truth is forever;
falsehood lasts but a moment.

Plot evil, and your heart drowns in deceit;
counsel peace, and you are filled with joy.

Act justly, and do not worry about consequences;
act wickedly, and fear every turn.

Dishonesty exiles you from God;
speak truth, and God will seek you out.

The wise value silence;
the ignorant prefer to babble.

Diligence is its own reward;
the dreams of the lazy die at dawn.

12:25

Do not surrender to worry;
do good, and worry surrenders to joy.

12:26

The wise overlook the foibles of others;
the wicked are obsessed by them.

12:27

Success through guile will not last;
wealth gained honestly endures forever.

12:28

Generosity is the way to life;
even death cannot block its path.

13:1-2

The wise child welcomes the advice of parents;
the wicked one ignores anything they suggest.

13:2

The wise are nourished by the fruit of their words,
but the wicked choke on violence.

13:3

Guard your tongue, and you guard your soul;
speak without reflection, and you invite disaster.

Lust drains the soul;
honest labor fills it to the brim.

The wise despise falsehood;
the wicked traffic therein.

Observe the truth, and the way is clear;
ignore it, and you lose direction.

Pretending to knowledge reveals your lack of it;
admitting ignorance is the beginning of wisdom.

Merit may be gained by generosity;
generosity without compassion is worth nothing.

The good are aflame with joy;
the lamp of the wicked is not yet lit.

A closed mind causes strife;
an open mind cultivates wisdom.

13:11

Easy money vanishes fast;
value comes from honest effort.

13:12

Breaking a promise causes heartache;
keeping a promise is a tree of life.

13:13

Belittling the truth invites trouble;
honoring the truth is its own reward.

13:14

The sage's teaching is a well of life;
its waters can save you from early death.

13:15

An attentive mind flourishes;
a distracted mind is barren.

13:16

Be wise and reflect before you act;
a fool follows every whim heedlessly.

13:17

One who is faithless will be betrayed;
one who is trustworthy invites the support of others.

One who lacks self-control is despised;
one who learns to curb desire is respected.

Detachment from desire frees the soul,
but the fool is a slave to every passion.

Walk with the wise, and gain wisdom;
keep company with fools, and you will regret it.

The evil are pursued by evil;
the good are rewarded with good.

The legacy of the wise is eternal,
the wicked leave nothing; even their merit is
    buried with them.

The poor labor hard and bring in the harvest,
but without justice they will reap no benefit.

Undisciplined parents produce unruly children;
good parents provide counsel and guidance.

13:25

The wise are satisfied with whatever they eat;
the wicked remain hungry no matter how much
they consume.

14:1

Wisdom sustains the home;
foolishness destroys it.

14:2

God is with those whose who walk straight;
wander from the path, and you are lost.

14:3

The arrogant choke on their own scorn;
the wise learn to restrain the tongue.

14:4

Without oxen the trough is clean, but there is
no harvest;
without discipline life seems easy, but there is
no wisdom.

14:5

Train yourself in honesty,
and your word will be trusted.

Liars are not believed even when they speak
   the truth;
those with integrity find discrimination easy.

Take nothing seriously,
and your lips will never know wisdom.

True wisdom is self-understanding;
fools deceive only themselves.

Foolish desires taste of guilt;
just desires are sweet on the tongue.

Only you know the bitterness in your heart,
and no stranger can sweeten it for you.

A strong fortress built on dishonesty will fall;
a flimsy tent pitched on justice will hold.

The shortest route is not always the best;
sometimes it leads to death.

14:13

Even good-natured teasing may cause distress;
be sure that laughter does not end in tears.

14:14

A heart filled with pride has lost its way;
the good learn to rise above it.

14:15

The ignorant believe every rationalization;
the wise consider every word.

14:16

The wise recognize their anger and hold it
    in check;
the ignorant use anger to justify their actions.

14:17

A short temper enslaves you;
those who procrastinate are disliked.

14:18

Fools inherit folly;
the wise invest in knowledge.

14:19

The wicked may prosper, yet the wise do not
    envy them;
wisdom always rules over wealth.

Even the poor ignore the poor,
but everyone seeks the company of the rich.

14:21

Those who neglect the poor betray the community;
only the generous are praiseworthy.

14:22

Sow evil and reap evil;
sow good and harvest mercy and truth.

14:23

Effort brings you joy;
idleness brings you sorrow.

14:24

The crown of the wise is their integrity;
the ignorant always dress in foolishness.

14:25

Truth saves lives;
self-deception destroys them.

14:26

Fear of God may keep you from error;
faith in God protects not only you but those
    you love.

14:27

Faith is the source of life,
diverting you from the snares of death.

14:28

The authority of kings comes from the people;
they have no power without a nation.

14:29

Patience is the sign of understanding;
a quick temper is the hallmark of a fool.

14:30

A calm mind refreshes the body;
jealousy disturbs you to your core.

14:31

Robbing the poor is an insult to God;
caring for the poor honors God.

14:32

The wicked are brought down by their evil;
the wise are protected by their integrity.

14:33

The wise heart is filled with tranquillity;
the foolish heart is ever on parade.

Generosity can save a nation,
but indiscriminate kindness can be harmful.

14:35

The wise serve others and are appreciated;
the self-absorbed are despised.

15:1

A gentle response defuses anger;
harsh words incite more rage.

15:2

The tongue of the wise imparts wisdom;
the mouth of the ignorant spreads folly.

15:3

You cannot escape from reality;
evil and good are visible to all.

15:4

Gentle encouragement is a tree of life;
critical words can murder the spirit.

15:5

The arrogant reject all guidance;
the wise treasure it and become wiser.

15:6

The house of the wise is strong,
but complacency can ruin its foundation.

15:7

The wise share their knowledge,
but angry hearts resent their efforts.

15:8

There is no reconciliation between good and evil;
therefore the wise pray for clarity.

15:9

Dishonesty is a betrayal of your birthright;
through discrimination freedom is found.

15:10

If you lack discipline, you reject good advice;
if you hate criticism, you are heading for disaster.

15:11

Never despair!
Redemption extends even beyond the grave.

15:12

The ignorant avoid the wise
and do not value their counsel.

15:13

Happiness illuminates the face;
misery shrouds the spirit.

15:14

A serious mind seeks understanding,
but a fool is satisfied with folly.

15:15

Those who envy are forever poor;
the generous never lack for anything.

15:16

Better a little earned honestly
than much won through deception.

15:17

Better a simple meal eaten with love
than a feast eaten in bitterness.

15:18

Anger engenders more anger;
patience leads to tranquillity.

15:19

The lazy path is strewn with thorns;
the way is clear for those who walk it
    purposefully.

15:20

A wise child is a father's delight;
a stupid child is a mother's shame.

15:21

The foolish heart is satisfied with folly;
the wise heart rejoices in justice.

15:22

Listen to no one, and you will fail;
hear what others have to say, and you will prosper.

15:23

An apt response is always welcome;
make sure your words fit the occasion.

15:24

The wise walk with purpose,
untroubled by impermanence or death.

15:25

The mansions of the arrogant will decay,
but the homes of the simple will last.

15:26

Evil thoughts pollute;
thoughtful words purify.

If wealth is ill-gotten,
even a palace is doomed.

Think before you speak;
the unrestrained tongue wreaks havoc.

Selfishness separates you from God;
selflessness awakens you to Him.

The truth gladdens the heart
and good news strengthens the bones.

Open your ears to guidance
and take your place among the wise.
Close your ears to counsel and you jeopardize
    your soul.
The wise heart welcomes truth.

The way to wisdom is through wonder;
the way to honor is through humility.

16:1

Your mind may be full of confusion,
but always speak as if talking to God.

16:2

Your mind can rationalize anything,
but your heart knows the truth.

16:3

Do whatever is kind,
and the way will become clear.

16:4

Everything is from God;
even evil plays a role in the divine drama.

16:5

Pride blinds you to the truth;
conceit corrupts every kindness.

16:6

If you turn from evil and stand in awe of God,
then your kindness and honesty will bring
    you forgiveness.

16:7

Align yourself with godliness,
and even your enemies will make peace with you.

PROVERBS

Righteousness alone determines the value of
    your work;
fame without justice is hollow.

Desire plots a course;
godliness secures the journey.

Charming words cannot mask evil acts;
you are judged according to your deeds.

Cosmic balance is in the hands of God;
be concerned only with your own integrity.

Take no pleasure in evil;
security lies with truth alone.

Wise leaders desire truth
and those who speak it are honored.

Anger has the power to destroy,
but the wise learn how to temper it.

16:15

The wise shed light on life;
their gifts are like rain falling on thirsty ground.

16:16

Seek wisdom over gold
and understanding more than silver.

16:17

Turn from evil, and your road is paved smoothly;
walk it, and your soul is protected.

16:18

Pride precedes a fall;
arrogance precedes a failure.

16:19

Better to be sad among the humble
than share the spoils of the proud.

16:20

What secures success?
Wise investigation and aligning yourself with
    goodness.

16:21

Be wise of heart and people will appreciate
    your understanding;

temper your speech and the wise will gladly
    teach you.

16:22

The wise seek wisdom as the source of life;
the schemes of the ignorant are shrouded
    in delusion.

16:23

A wise heart leads to right speech;
train your lips to speak the truth.

16:24

Gentle words are like a honeycomb,
sweet to the soul and healing to the body.

16:25

Be aware of the consequences of your actions:
some things seem right at first glance,
but in the end they lead to destruction.

16:26

The quest for wisdom is its own reward;
let your actions be driven by truth.

16:27

The careless stir up slander as if it were a treasure;
their lips burn with envy's fire.

16:28

A liar incites others to violence;
the grumbler alienates those who might be of help.

16:29

The violent arouse their friends
and lead them in the wrong direction.

16:30

If your eyes are closed to truth, you will be
    deceived.
If your mouth is always open, you may say things
    you regret.

16:31

Those who are honorable
will find old age the crown of their achievements.

16:32

Patience is the greatest strength,
self-control the key to success.

16:33

The odds are always at risk;
the outcome is known only by God.

17:1

Eating a crust of bread in peace
is better than feasting in a strife-torn house.

An intelligent nanny will discipline a naughty
   child
and earn the love that is her due.

A refining pot tries silver,
a crucible tries gold,
but only God can try the heart.

No matter what is said, the troublemaker hears
   evil;
no matter how true it is, the liar believes it to
   be false.

Mock the poor, and you insult the Creator;
rejoice at others' misfortune, and you will suffer.

Grandchildren are a delight to old people;
parents are a joy to their children.

A liar who speaks the truth will not be believed;
falsehood is alien to those who are honest.

17:8

People who give bribes are deluded;
they imagine their success is secured.

17:9

Those who forgive insults keep their friends;
those who harp on faults are lonely.

17:10

The wise learn something from every mistake;
the fool learns nothing from a hundred errors.

17:11

Those who seek profit through deceit
are cheated by those with whom they do business.

17:12

It is easier to deal with an angry bear
than a fool convinced of his foolishness.

17:13

If you repay good with evil,
evil will take root in your home.

17:14

Starting a quarrel is like opening a floodgate;
abandon the thought before you drown in anger.

Rationalizing evil and condemning good
both pervert the way of godliness.

Wealthy fools can afford teachers,
but they are too opinionated to heed them.

A friend's love is always available,
but siblings are there in times of trouble.

Friendship may vanish
if you become business partners.

Betrayal breeds violence;
arrogance invites its own destruction.

A twisted heart cannot fathom goodness;
a lying tongue cannot speak truth.

Encourage crime, and fear haunts you;
allow others to be shamed, and joy escapes you.

17:22

A glad heart is sure medicine,
despair a cancer to the bone.

17:23

The wicked are quick to bribe
in order to divert the course of justice.

17:24

The wise find wisdom everywhere;
the ignorant look for it somewhere else.

17:25

Parents fret over their children's mistakes;
this causes churning in their souls.

17:26

The dishonest hate those who obey the law
and envy those who are generous to others.

17:27

Silence is a hallmark of wisdom;
the words of the wise are few.

17:28

Even fools can hold their tongues;
sealed lips do not always mean an understanding
    heart.

Do not fall prey to desire
for you will be disgraced among your peers.

The ignorant express a desire for wisdom
only when their ignorance is exposed.

Contempt travels with evil;
insult accompanies disgrace.

The mouth is like the source of a great river;
its words can irrigate or flood.

Returning evil with kindness is not good,
for how then will you honor kindness?

Foolish words attract contention;
foolish acts invite violence.

Foolish words bring disaster
and cause your soul to falter.

18:8

Whining is like a hammer;
its pounding shatters the heart.

18:9

If you are lax in your discipline,
you contribute to your own destruction.

18:10

Surrendering to God is the key to endurance;
this way you will finish the course.

18:11

Do not belittle wealth;
it can be a source of strength in time of trouble.

18:12

The arrogant teeter on the brink of destruction;
the humble stand at the threshold of honor.

18:13

Offering advice before listening carefully
is both stupid and useless.

18:14

A joyous heart strengthens the body;
despair exposes it to every disease.

Intuition is a source of knowledge,
but do not forsake reason in your quest for truth.

Generosity opens many doors;
even the famous welcome the openhearted.

Do not be the first person to complain;
wait until you have heard what others have to say.

The toss of a coin can sometimes end quarrels
and send the contentious on their way.

Even quarreling brothers and sisters
will often come to each other's defense.

The satisfaction of your soul
depends upon the quality of your words.

Death and life lie in the power of words;
Hasty speech may mean you have to eat your
    words later.

18:22

A loving partner is a source of happiness;
God smiles on the union of such souls.

18:23

When you ask for a favor, speak gently;
keep your words soft no matter how harsh
    the response.

18:24

Friends may be closer than siblings,
for friendship rests on a foundation of trust
    not blood.

19:1

Better a pauper on the path of innocence
than a rich person on the road to corruption.

19:2

Hearts empty of understanding have nothing
    to offer;
leaping without looking can carry you toward evil.

19:3

Ignorance is corrupting;
embrace it, and your heart will rage against justice.

19:4

Wealth attracts many followers;
poverty can separate you even from your friends.

19:5

Bearing false witness cannot be excused;
lying invites its own consequences.

19:6

The poor are drawn to the generous;
even the wealthy honor one who gives freely.

19:7

A despairing heart drives away friends;
when it cries out, it speaks only to itself.

19:8

True understanding brings self-esteem;
happiness arises in a heart fulfilled.

19:9

A false witness stands self-condemned;
liars are trapped by their own lies.

19:10

Privilege is wasted on the ignorant
for their desires are insatiable.

Patience is a sign of intelligence;
honor comes to those who do not take offense.

The ignorant rampage like young lions;
their attention lasts no longer than dew on the grass.

An unruly child causes heartache;
a nagging spouse is like a dripping tap.

Property and wealth can be inherited,
but a wise spouse is a gift from God.

Laziness leads to neglect;
idle minds receive no nourishment.

Doing what needs to be done is a boon to
    the soul;
ignoring responsibility is the way of death.

When you give to the poor, imagine you are
    giving to God;
your reward will be instantaneous.

Hope requires curbing desire;
self-indulgence is the path to destruction.

Angry people cause their own problems;
trying to intervene only fuels their anger.

Welcome advice and discipline when you
    are young;
they will bring wisdom when you are older.

Your mind is filled with many dreams,
yet life unfolds despite them.

Better to befriend an honest pauper
than kneel before a treacherous king.

The key to life is attention to the truth;
the godly die in peace and their mistakes are
    forgotten.

You may be holding food in your hand,
but you will starve unless you put it in your mouth.

THE FIRST COLLECTION OF SHORTER SAYINGS

19:25

Discipline the cynical, and they grow clever;
discipline the wise, and they grow wiser.

19:26

Security and independence mean nothing
to parents whose children are delinquent.

19:27

Attending to reality returns your feet to the path
and your mind to the present moment.

19:28–29

Criminals mock justice and lie about their
    activities,
but retribution will catch up with them; there is
    no escape.

20:1

Wine loosens the tongue and causes trouble;
this is not the path of discrimination.

20:2

Do not provoke the king's anger;
treat him as you would a raging lion.

20:3

Avoiding an argument is a wise choice;
a hasty retort is a sign of stupidity.

The lazy shirk their responsibilities when times
    are hard,
then expect to harvest what they did not sow.

Understanding is a deep river running through
    the heart;
learn to draw from it, and you will grow wise.

Most people claim to be kind,
but the truth is known through their deeds.

Good citizens are full of integrity;
those who follow their leadership are fortunate.

A discerning mind recognizes what is false
by simply observing the situation.

There is no permanent state of purity;
do not imagine your heart is pure and your
    errors erased.

20:10

Cheating customers and stealing from owners
cheapen the value of honest labor.

20:11

Youth is no excuse;
goodness and justice are for everyone.

20:12

The ear is for listening, not just hearing;
the eye for seeing, not just looking.

20:13

Those who prefer illusion impoverish their souls;
the awakened eye sees riches wherever it rests.

20:14

Do not complain about how others do business,
then boast to your friends of your own
cleverness.

20:15

Gold and pearls are worth nothing
when compared to right speech.

20:16

Obtain collateral from anyone cosigning for
a stranger
or vouching for someone you do not know.

The bread of falsehood tastes sweet at first;
once chewed it turns to gravel in your mouth.

Make sure to seek objective counsel
when planning strategies for success.

Beware of mingling among the indiscreet
or with those who gossip and tell lies.

Blaming your parents keeps you from tending your
    own flame;
when night falls, you will be lost in darkness.

Do not rush to enjoy what comes easily;
make sure the blessing does not disguise a curse.

Do not dedicate your life to revenge;
surrender your revenge to God.

Do not deceive those who trust you;
anything less than an honest measure is wrong.

20:24

Each step is taken in the company of God,
if you understand the nature of the journey.

20:25

Injustice and lies lead you from the path;
honesty and generosity return you to it.

20:26

A wise leader knows how to quell troublemakers
and turn their mischief against them.

20:27

The soul is a lamp that illuminates
the dark corners of mind and heart.

20:28

Kindness and truth sustain you on the path;
through these you will be strengthened.

20:29

The young take pride in their youth;
the old find value in aging.

20:30

Punishment may reform the criminal;
the wise are guided by the gnawing of
    conscience.

Like a farmer irrigating his fields,
let truth direct the desires of your heart.

It is easy to rationalize your actions;
look for the truth buried beneath your excuses.

Doing what is right and just
is true service to God.

A disdainful attitude and a proud heart
sow the seeds of discord.

Although at the beginning your thoughts are
    pure and good,
hasty action may result in loss.

Ill-gotten gains are like poisoned perfume;
attraction to either leads to death.

Those who are not honest with themselves are
    like thieves
whose lives are blighted by fear.

21:8

Even if your actions are sometimes inconsistent,
make sure they are always straightforward.

21:9

Living alone in the corner of an attic
is better than sharing a large space with a difficult
    spouse.

21:10

A warped mind looks for trouble;
even friends are sacrificed to achieve its aims.

21:11

Punishment may teach some people;
the wise gain knowledge through instruction.

21:12

Even the wicked prosper;
they credit their good fortune to evil.

21:13

Ignore the cry of the needy,
and your own cries will be ignored.

21:14

Giving anonymously to the poor frees you
    from anger;
generosity is an antidote to wrath.

PROVERBS

Just deeds bring joy
and destroy the workings of iniquity.

Wander off the path of wisdom,
and you will find yourself among dead souls.

Devoting yourself to pleasure will leave you
    penniless;
indulge in wine and perfume, and poverty
    awaits you.

Traps are set for the righteous,
but it is the wicked who fall into them.

Better to pitch your tent in a wasteland
than live with a violent and angry spouse.

The wise conserve what they have;
the ignorant squander their inheritance and
    become poor.

21:21

Do good and be kind,
and strength and honor will follow you.

21:22

The mind controls the body;
place your trust in wisdom, not strength.

21:23

Guard your tongue,
and you protect your soul.

21:24

Those who impose their will on others
fall prey to arrogance and evil.

21:25

Laziness will overcome you
if you resist every impulse to work.

21:26

The ignorant dream and accomplish nothing;
the wise act to the benefit of both self and other.

21:27

Whatever the ignorant have to offer,
they will use to their own advantage.

False testimony may be refuted,
but once it is voiced, everyone repeats it.

Know-it-alls display their ignorance;
the wise trust in not knowing.

Cultivate wisdom and understanding,
and destructive thoughts will not lead to harmful
    action.

Saddle your horse for battle,
but never take victory for granted.

Your good name is your greatest treasure;
your reputation more precious than silver or gold.

Don't praise the rich or condemn the poor;
they are both equal in God's eyes.

The wise recognize trouble and avoid it;
the thoughtless do not notice and pay dearly.

22:4

Humility brings you into God's presence,
and with this comes wealth, honor, and vitality.

22:5

The path of the ignorant is strewn with thorns
    and snares;
the wise choose not to walk this way.

22:6

Teach people the truth when they are young,
and they will not abandon it even in old age.

22:7

The rich dominate the poor,
and the debtor is bound to the creditor.

22:8

Sow injustice and reap disaster;
anger will burn up your inheritance.

22:9

Blessed are those who give bread to the poor,
looking beyond their poverty to their divinity.

22:10

Put an end to sarcasm and ridicule,
and judgment and shame will also cease.

One who has a pure heart and kind speech
dwells in the company of God.

22:12

God protects knowledge;
honesty reveals the words of the liar.

22:13

The lazy imagine stalking lions,
then cower from their own fantasies.

22:14

The mouth that utters falsehood
will swallow the one who speaks it.

22:15

If you are tied to the illusion of words,
only silence can separate you from it.

22:16

Whatever you think to gain from exploitation
will ultimately be counted as a loss.

The Thirty Precepts of Wisdom

PROLOGUE

22:17–21

Concentrate on the words of the wise,
and establish your heart in truth.
Repeating the words of the wise
will protect you from wrongdoing.
Trust in God, even if you feel unworthy.
I will now describe the path you should follow.
Here in writing are the principles of knowledge
    that you need.
I have written down the elements of truth
so that you will be able to teach other seekers.

THE THIRTY PRECEPTS

22:22–23

Do not exploit the defenseless,
nor take advantage of the poor,
for God will come to their rescue,
stripping from you what you planned to steal
    from them.

22:24–25

Do not entertain anger
or be tempted by rage.
The more you lose your temper,
the more you become its slave.

22:26–27

Do not rush to make a deal
or guarantee a loan.
If you cannot afford to lose money,
do not risk the very bed you sleep on.

Do not discount the wisdom of the past;
it may save you from trouble in the present.

A hard worker can stand tall before kings;
there is no greater honor than honest labor.

Be wary when dining with the powerful;
think carefully before opening your mouth.
If it helps, imagine a knife at your throat,
and keep your appetite under control.
Don't envy their rich food;
their cake may be laced with deceit.

Do not berate yourself for having less;
take comfort in your own understanding.
Money comes when it comes, and then it
    disappears,
like an eagle soaring high in the heavens.

Do not break bread with the mean-spirited,
nor envy their possessions.
They will tally up each mouthful of food.

Eat! Drink! they insist, but they don't really
    mean it.
The bread of the stingy will turn in your
    stomach,
and your expression of thanks will stick in
    your craw.

23:9

Don't waste words on those who plug their ears;
they will not value what you have to say.

23:10–12

Do not steal from the defenseless;
they are protected by God.
Open your heart to correction
and your ears to knowledge.

23:13–14

Do not give in to the temptations of youth;
discipline will not kill you.
Make every effort to resist
and keep your soul from lasting guilt.

23:15–16

A wise heart brings joy to others;
they will yearn for your good counsel.

Do not envy those who worship pleasure;
try to be mindful of God all day.
Godliness is all that lasts;
faith in it is never misplaced.

Listen to me and grow wise;
follow what you know in your heart.
Do not go out drinking every night,
nor keep company with the greedy.
Wine and meat will drain your reserves;
drowsiness will overcome you.

By all means buy books,
but do not reduce wisdom, discipline, and
    understanding to commodities.

Always listen to your father
and honor your mother no matter how old
    she grows.
The father of the wise is happy;
the mother of the wise rejoices.

Become wise, and those who raised you will
    celebrate.

23:26–28

Turn your heart to wisdom,
and your eyes will be drawn to the good.
Lust is a deep pit, and evil passion a narrow well;
fall into either one, and you are trapped.

23:29–35

Observe those who are devoted
to quarreling, idle talk, and fighting.
They linger over wine
and indulge themselves with strong liquor.
You will not discover truth at the bottom of a
    wine glass.
An alcoholic loses his grasp on reality
as surely as death comes from a sudden snakebite.
If you drink like this, you will hallucinate and the
    world will appear distorted.
Everything will lurch up and down like a raft on
    the high seas.
You claim that wine is medicine,
that it will be your salvation,

but when you are sober, you will long for more wine
and the madness you now call sanity.

24:1–2

Do not admire mischief makers, nor seek out
their company.
They are up to no good and are always
discontented.

24:3–4

A true home is built on wisdom, with a firm
foundation of understanding.
Knowledge gives each room a deep tranquillity.

24:5–6

The wise are steadfast and fortified by knowledge.
Their plans come to fruition and their counsel
is useful.

24:7

To the ignorant wisdom makes no sense;
they do not know enough to ask for help.

24:8–9

Allow your mind to be seduced, and you will
make mistakes.
Distraction leads away from truth; cynicism will
cripple you.

24:10

Do not plead weakness when someone needs you;
eventually your own strength will fail you.

24:11–12

If innocent people are murdered and you do
    nothing,
it is no good pleading ignorance.
God sees the situation clearly.
The moment will come when you are in danger,
and your inaction will be repaid by the inaction
    of others.

24:13–14

You eat honey for its simple goodness
and its sweet taste on your tongue.
So let it be with wisdom, for it, too, is good
    and offers you the sweetness of hope.

24:15–16

Wickedness disturbs tranquillity.
Goodness may fall seven times but recovers eight;
evil stumbles once and is destroyed.

24:17–18

Do not gloat when criminals are caught and
    punished.

Their punishment is not for your pleasure,
and your enjoyment may change the course
of events.

Do not rail against the wicked,
nor envy what they do.
They leave nothing behind,
and their lamp is extinguished forever.

24:21–22

Respect both God and the king,
but choose the former over the latter.
Do not trust those who cannot decide between
piety and power.
Calamity fells them suddenly,
and who knows whether this comes from God
or the king?

THE THIRTY PRECEPTS OF WISDOM

Sayings of Solomon's Contemporaries

24:23

These are the sayings of the sages (compiled
    by Solomon):

If you have to make a judgment, show no
    favoritism.

24:24–25

Those who judge what is right as wrong will
    be shunned,
and everyone will avoid their company.
If you have to sentence someone, do it firmly
    but kindly
and you will be respected.

24:26

Always speak honestly and directly,
and people will receive what you say as though
    it were a kiss.

24:27

Before embarking on family life,
make sure that you can afford to support those you
will come to love.

24:28

Do not let your feelings for one friend
persuade you to betray another.

24:29

Do not feel indebted
to one who cheats on your behalf.

24:30–31

What does laziness accomplish?
Look at the fields and vineyards of the idle.
They are overgrown with thistles,
the ground is covered with nettles, stone walls no
longer stand.

24:32–34

Observe this and see what it teaches you.
The lazy curl up in bed: a little more sleep,
another short nap;
poverty sneaks up on them and robs them of all
they have.

The Second Collection of Shorter Sayings

25:1

Here are further sayings of Solomon
collected by the scribes of Hezekiah, king
    of Judah:

25:2

In matters of the spirit metaphor is used;
in matters of state it is better to speak plainly.

25:3

As unfathomable as heaven's height and earth's
    depth
is the heart of a wise leader.

25:4–5

Just as dross must be removed from silver
before it can be refined into a cup,
so wickedness must be driven from a nation
if its leaders are to govern with integrity.

Do not boast to curry favor with the powerful.

Let them invite you to join them of their own
accord.

If you overstate your case, you may be demoted
later.

Do not get involved in an argument
unless the whole matter is clear.

Do not betray a confidence in the heat of the
moment;

you may be overheard and lose your reputation
forever.

Like golden apples engraved on silver plates
is a well-timed word of advice.

Like a nose ring of gold or precious brooch
is wise counsel in a receptive ear.

Like cooling snow during winter's harvest
is one who keeps a promise that refreshes the spirit.

Like empty clouds and hot dry winds
is one whose promises are hollow.

Do not be impatient with the powerful;
respond gently to their anger.

When you find honey, eat only what you need;
any more will sour your stomach.

Tread softly in a friend's house,
for even friendship has its limits.

False testimony is as deadly
as any weapon.

Like a broken tooth or sprained ankle
is trust betrayed in a time of need.

Like a thin cloak in winter or wine mixed
    with vinegar
is a song of joy to a saddened heart.

If your enemy is hungry—bring food. If thirsty—
    bring water.
Your actions may shame your adversary into a
    change of heart.

As sure as the north wind brings rain,
slander calls forth anger.

Better to live in the corner of the attic
than deal with an angry spouse among friends.

Like cold water to a thirsty traveler
is good news from far away.

Like a muddied spring or poisoned well
is one who fails to withstand corruption.

Honey and honor are both sweet,
but too much of either will make you sick.

Like a city whose walls lie in ruin
is one whose desires are not curbed.

Like summer snow and winter rain,
honors showered on the ignorant wreak havoc.

Like a swallow flying back to its nest,
harsh words will haunt their author.

A whip for the horse, a bridle for the donkey,
and a sharp reproof for the fool.

Do not humor the ignorant,
or you will appear as witless as they do.

Answer a fool according to his foolishness,
and he may mistake his ignorance for wisdom.

Sending messages through fools
results in confusion, anger, and misunderstanding.

A parable from the lips of the ignorant
is as useless as shoes on a man without legs.

26:8

Honoring the ignorant is like loading a stone
into a sling:
disaster is bound to follow.

26:9

A thorn in the hand of a drunk causes as
much trouble
as a parable told by a fool.

26:10

A undisciplined boss creates confusion
by hiring unqualified and dishonest people.

26:11

Someone who keeps making the same mistakes
is like a dog sniffing its own vomit.

26:12

Better to believe that you are ignorant
than pretend to yourself that you are wise.

26:13

The lazy invent excuses to avoid work:
How can I go out? A lion is loose in the streets.

26:14

As a door turns on its hinge,
so the lazy turn on their beds.

The lazy cannot feed themselves
even when the food is placed in their hands.

The ignorant believe themselves wiser
than seven others with more knowledge.

Like a person pinching the ear of an angry dog
is one who gets embroiled in another's quarrel.

Like a warrior probing for an army's weakness
is one who lies and says *I'm only joking.*

Wood fuels fire,
and sharp words an argument.

Like a flame to dying embers
is a troublemaker to a cooling temper.

The words of a complainer
churn the stomachs of those to whom they speak.

26:22

Like cheap spoons covered with silver plate
are kind words concealing mean intentions.

26:23

Deceitful words pretend to honesty,
but secretly they harbor fraud.

26:24

The speech of the untrustworthy may be gentle,
but their hearts are hard with malice.

26:25

No matter how pleasant a person's voice,
look to deeds when deciding whom to trust.

26:26

Though criminals may nurse their grievances
    in private,
their anger is revealed in public.

26:27

Set a trap, and you will be caught in it;
roll a stone to crush another, and it will fall on you.

26:28

Hatred feeds upon hatred;
respond gently, and hatred may soften.

Do not be certain of tomorrow;
no one knows what the future will bring.

Let your praise come from others, not yourself;
from strangers and not from your own lips.

A boulder is heavy and sacks of sand are hard
    to lift,
but senseless anger weighs more than both.

Hatred breeds cruelty and rage smolders,
but envy is the hardest to uproot.

Even a public rebuke is acceptable
if you know it is fueled by love.

Criticism from a friend is useful,
but support by an enemy is useless.

A tranquil mind curbs desire;
a disturbed mind even mistakes the bitter
    for sweet.

THE SECOND COLLECTION OF SHORTER SAYINGS

27:8

Like a bird forced from its nest
is a mind unable to be tranquil.

27:9

Perfume and incense gladden the heart,
but not as much as the counsel of a good friend.

27:10

Do not forsake your friends,
nor the friends of your parents.
Do not seek help from a sibling far away;
a close neighbor is as good as a distant relative.

27:11

A child's wisdom gladdens a parent's heart
and staves off all humiliation.

27:12

A shrewd person sees trouble coming and avoids it;
the ignorant walk right into it and pay the price.

27:13

Seek collateral from those
who cosign for strangers and foreigners.

27:14

One who talks about others' generosity
invites thieves into their house.

Living with a crabby spouse is like being locked in
a room
with a leaky roof on a rainy day.

Denying your spouse's anger is as impossible
as ignoring the wind or concealing the aroma
of a perfumed hand.

As iron sharpens iron,
so friends sharpen the minds of friends.

Whoever tends a fig tree eats of its fruit;
so one who guards a friend's reputation is
also honored.

As water reflects back your face,
let your heart mirror the face of a friend.

Like graveyards and Hell,
the wandering eye is never satisfied.

27:21

As a refining pot clarifies silver and a crucible
    purifies gold,
so what you value reveals your true nature.

27:22

Even if the ignorant were grain,
no mortar and pestle could grind their ignorance
    out of them.

27:23

Get to know those who work for you,
and delegate responsibility only to those you trust.

27:24

Strength does not last forever,
nor wealth outlive its heirs.

27:25

Know that both profit and loss come to all
    who labor;
sometimes the mountains bloom, sometimes
    the hills are barren.

27:26

Let your own effort clothe you;
value your labor as you would a prized possession.

Do not spend more than you can afford,
and do not marry off your children for profit.

The ignorant run from imagined fears,
while the wise are as confident as strong lions.

Greedy developers exploit the land;
good citizens preserve it.

A poor man who robs the destitute
is like a monsoon that destroys the crops.

Those who forsake wisdom side with the ignorant,
but the wise stand against them.

Ignorance blinds us to the consequences of
    our actions;
wisdom opens everything to understanding.

Better the poor who are innocent
than the rich who twist the ways of justice.

28:7

Those who honor wisdom honor their parents;
those who become drunkards humiliate them.

28:8

The profits of a loan shark
will end up in the pockets of the poor.

28:9

The prayers of those deaf to wisdom
fall on deaf ears.

28:10

Trip up those who are honest, and you yourself
    will stumble.
The inheritance of innocence is goodness.

28:11

Wealthy people who become self-satisfied
are poorer than those who possess only self-
    knowledge.

28:12

When the good triumph, there is great rejoicing;
when the wicked succeed, no one applauds.

28:13

Hide your wrongdoing, and you will be exposed;
repent your mistakes, and you will be forgiven.

The wise avoid mistakes by taking thought;
the self-important rush toward disaster.

Like a roaring lion and an angry bear,
the wicked attack the defenseless.

A ignorant prince invites invasion;
a wise leader governs in peace.

A murderer will run until exhausted;
no one will offer sanctuary.

The innocent are saved by their simplicity;
the devious are entrapped by their own cunning.

Work the land and harvest bread;
pursue vanity and reap stones.

A life of integrity is its own blessing;
those impatient for success will end up with
nothing.

28:21

Don't take sides in judging the guilty;
the hungry may steal bread in order to live.

28:22

The eye of the greedy is blind
and cannot discern what is to come.

28:23

The wise know who their friends are:
the counselors, not the flatterers.

28:24

Children who steal from their parents claiming
    it is their inheritance
are no better than criminals.

28:25

The greedy are rewarded with trouble;
those who trust in truth have abundance.

28:26

The ignorant succumb to their every desire;
the wise escape calamity through discrimination.

28:27

One who gives generously receives generously;
one who ignores the poor courts disaster.

When the wicked rule, people hide;
when they are overthrown, the righteous inherit.

The arrogant ignore every warning;
they break their necks because of their rigid
    position.

Happiness abounds when the righteous rule,
but misery is audible in the land of the wicked.

Seekers of wisdom are a blessing to their family;
lovers of sex will squander their inheritance.

Justice establishes a nation;
graft destroys it.

Deceive someone by flattery,
and you will be deceived in the same manner.

The wicked are ensnared by their own schemes;
the good sing and are glad.

29:7

The righteous attend to the needs of the poor;
the wicked have no comprehension of justice.

29:8

Cynics can inflame a city,
but the wise know how to cool anger.

29:9

The wise who enter into an argument with fools
find that neither anger nor humor can resolve
    the matter.

29:10

The violent despise the innocent;
the wise seek their company.

29:11

The ignorant express their anger;
the wise know how to hold their tongues.

29:12

When an employer is open to gossip,
every employee becomes a tattletale.

29:13

The greedy ignore the poor and the broken,
pretending their fate is the will of God.

A leader who treats the destitute fairly
will be remembered by posterity.

Discipline results in wisdom;
self-indulgence is a disgrace to the whole family.

Though the wicked may prosper from their
    wickedness,
the righteous will outlast them.

Teaching your children self-control
will bring peace and delight to your heart.

Without vision a nation disintegrates,
but those who adhere to truth are praised.

Words alone cannot bring self-control;
understanding is not enough to break a bad habit.

There is more hope for a fool
than for those who act without thinking.

Indulge your desires in your youth,
and they will enslave you in old age.

Anger provokes violence;
uncontrolled rage destroys all hope of reconciliation.

Pride brings you low;
humility raises you up.

Side with thieves, and your conscience will be
    stolen;
You may lie even in a court of law.

If you fear others, your fear will entrap you;
if you trust in God, you will be safe.

Many curry favor with the rich,
but true judgment comes from God.

Criminals are anathema to the law-abiding;
they who are honest are an affront to those who
    break the law.

Warnings and Numerical Proverbs

30:1–4

These are the words of the Doubter:

There is no God, and we can know nothing of
godliness.

We are mere beasts, lacking any understanding.

We have not mastered wisdom, nor are we privy to divine
revelation.

Who among us can ascend to heaven and return with
wisdom?

Who can gather the wind in the palm of a hand?

Who can catch up the waters in a cloak?

Who can set the boundaries of the earth?

What is this person's name?

Does she have children? What are their names?

Tell if you know!

These are the words of the Knower:

Every word I speak is honed by God.
God is my shield from delusion.
I warn you: Do not add to the word of God;
your lies will be tested and exposed.
I ask but two things of God.
May they be granted before I die:
Keep me from vanity and falsehood, wealth and
    poverty;
provide me with a little bread each day,
just enough to sustain me.
Any more, and I may imagine it my own doing;
any less, and I may turn to theft and lies.

Speak no slander—not even against the wicked
who curse their fathers or neglect their mothers;
who believe themselves to be so pure that they fail
    to cleanse their hearts;
whose eyes blaze with disdain and whose brows
    arch with scorn;
whose teeth are swords and knives devouring the
    land of the poor

and depriving the destitute of sanctuary.

For so poisonous is slander that in the end it is the
slanderer who will be called wicked.

30:15a

Death has two insatiable daughters:

Eden says: *Give me the good.*

Hell says: *Let me swallow the wicked.*

30:15b–16

There are three things that are never satisfied,
truly four that never say *enough!*

The grave, a barren womb, parched land, and
fire—these are never satisfied.

30:17

The eye that mocks its father and scorns its mother

is plucked out by ravens and consumed by young
eagles.

30:18–19

There are three things beyond my comprehension;
a fourth thing, too, is beyond my ken:
the flight of an eagle in the sky;
the slithering of a serpent over a rock;
the course of a ship in the midst of the ocean;
and the passionate love of two young people.

WARNINGS AND NUMERICAL PROVERBS

Those who gorge on evil
and wipe their lips saying *I've done no wrong,*
their deeds are known to God.

Three things disturb the natural order
and bring trembling to the earth,
a fourth she cannot bear:
a slave who becomes a slave master;
a liar who lays claim to honesty;
a slut who pretends to modesty;
a maid who marries her mistress's husband.

There are four creatures whose instincts should
    guide us:
ants are a nation of little strength, yet they are
    always prepared for winter;
rabbits are not mighty, yet they make their home
    in the rocks;
locusts have no king, yet when they swarm they
    do so as one;
spiders may live in palaces, yet they are not too
    proud to catch their own food.

There are three who sleep securely,
a fourth who walks with confidence:
The lion is the strongest of creatures and is not
    afraid of anything,
the greyhound,
the billy goat,
and the king whose armies repel aggression.

If you have been hurt,
do not give in to anger
and silence thoughts of revenge.
Just as churning milk produces butter
and twisting someone's nose causes bleeding,
so nursing anger ends in violence.

A Mother's Advice

31:1-2

The advice of a mother, a solemn warning to her
    child:
I raised you and bore you and vowed all my love
    to you—
so listen, my child, to my advice:

31:3

Do not be carried away by passion
nor enslaved by power.

31:4-7

Drunkenness and alcoholism are not appropriate
    for the godly.
Neither wine nor beer befits one who seeks the
    truth.
Strong drink clouds the mind
and leads to the corruption of justice for the poor.

Yet a little beer may be a balm to the lost and
   those whose souls are bitter.
Do not judge the suffering who drink for a
   moment's respite.

31:8–9

Open your mouth and speak for those who have
   no voice;
seek justice for those who have no champion.
Open your mouth and plead for the rights
of those who are poor and needy.

31:10–31

A woman of great accomplishment,
who is worthy of her?
Her value is far beyond pearls.
She guides her husband's heart, and through her
   wisdom the household flourishes.
She repays kindness with more kindness and is
   never driven to revenge.
She buys wool and flax and works cheerfully in
   her home.
She fills herself with wisdom from far-off lands,
   like a merchant ship laden with treasure.

She rises early to attend to her household, her
family, and her servants.

She plans her expenditure with care; she buys land
and plants a vineyard.

She is a tower of strength, her arms strong and secure.

She devotes herself to what is useful and lets
nothing snuff out her lamp.

She reaches for the spinning wheel and cradles the
spindle in her palm.

She opens her hands to the poor and her arms to
comfort the needy.

She fears no winter, for she has clothed her
household in scarlet wool.

She makes for herself glorious bedspreads and
dresses of fine linen and purple wool.

She counsels her husband, and her knowledge
makes him wise among the elders.

She weaves cloth and sells cloaks and belts to
peddlers.

She adorns herself with dignity and is not afraid
of the truth.

Her speech is full of wisdom; her tongue teaches
human kindness.

She anticipates the needs of her household and
    does not eat the bread of laziness.
Each morning her children feel blessed; her
    husband praises her saying:
There are many wonderful women, but you surpass
    them all.
Do not be taken in by grace and beauty alone;
praise only the woman who devotes herself to God.
The way she lives is evidence of her integrity;
her whole life is a testimony to her goodness.

THE BOOK OF PROVERBS is a three-thousand-year-old how-to manual. It was perhaps the first of what has proven to be an inexhaustible genre. Go to any well-stocked bookstore and browse the self-help section. You will find dozens and dozens of books explaining how to make yourself thinner, smarter, sexier, happier, richer, and more powerful. But there are few, if any, that offer to make you wiser. Why are so many devoted to the outer you and so few to the inner you? Because it is easier to change the mask we wear than the face that wears it.

Solomon is guiding us in the discipline of the mind and spirit. He is not interested in our happiness or our social rank. And while he does believe that the wise are happier than the ignorant, happi-

ness is a by-product of his primary concern—
wisdom.

Wisdom in the Book of Proverbs is not an
abstraction. It is a guiding principle. It is not a
matter of knowledge alone but of applying knowledge to our everyday lives. Solomon urges us to
act rather than react; to forge our own way in
the world rather than give in to laziness and glut-
tony. Solomon wants us to be the person we
were meant to be: strong, fair, honest, courageous,
kind, generous, and mindful of the One Who is
our source and substance.

I have long felt it is a shame that in most book-
stores the Bible sections are categorized as religion
rather than self-help. The Bible isn't about religion.
Yes, it contains instructions for those who wish to
participate in the religious cult of the ancient
Hebrews, but the best parts of the Bible are not
levitical rulings but guidelines for righteous living.

Are the grand narratives of the Bible a religion?

Are the Ten Commandments a religion?

Is the holiness code of Leviticus 19 that tells us
to love our neighbor as ourselves a religion?

Are the Psalms a religion?

No. Religion is about power and priestcraft. Religion has an in-group and an out-group. Religion has rules, the violation of which incurs the wrath and punishment of the pious elite.

Is there anything in the Book of Proverbs that speaks of this? No. Solomon speaks to all people at all times. There are no chosen and no damned. There are the wise and the ignorant; the diligent and the lazy; the intelligent and the fool. Are we not all of these at times?

The Book of Proverbs speaks of people and life; it speaks to people who wish to live well and find true satisfaction and tranquillity. It is a how-to book. But unlike most such books, it is not given to easy recipes. Solomon does not prescribe exactly what we need to do, but rather shares with us timeless principles that we can put into practice. We are all individuals. We cannot be reduced to a single prescription. But we can share a common set of principles. Our uniqueness is preserved in the way we apply the wisdom of Solomon, for no two of us will apply it in exactly the same way.

I hope that if you are reading the final pages of this book, you have already read those that precede it. You have read and pondered, at least for a while, the challenge of Solomon's proverbs and guidance. I urge you not to put this book aside. Rather, now that you have some familiarity with the text, reread it with even greater concentration. Take one teaching at a time and ask yourself, How can I apply this principle in my life? How can I take upon myself the discipline of wisdom, the instruction of she who calls to me from within Solomon's words?

Solomon has given voice to wisdom. You must give her legs.

Rabbi Rami M. Shapiro is regarded as one of the most creative voices in contemporary American Judaism. He is an award-winning poet and essayist and his liturgies are used in prayer services throughout North America. Rabbi Shapiro is a graduate of the Hebrew Union College Jewish Institute of Religion and holds a doctoral degree in religious studies from Union Graduate School. A congregational rabbi for twenty years, he is currently the president of Metivta, a center for contemplative Judaism in Los Angeles, and director of the Simply Jewish Foundation (www.simplyjewish.com). His most recent books are *Minyan: Ten Principles for Living a Life of Integrity*, *Wisdom of the Jewish Sages: A Modern Reading of* Pirke Avot, and *The Way of Solomon: Finding Joy and Contentment in the Wisdom of* Ecclesiastes.

OTHER BELL TOWER BOOKS

*Books that nourish the soul, illuminate the mind,
and speak directly to the heart*

Rob Baker
PLANNING MEMORIAL CELEBRATIONS
A Sourcebook

A one-stop handbook for a situation more and more of us are
facing as we grow older. / 0-609-80404-9 · *Softcover*

Thomas Berry
THE GREAT WORK
Our Way into the Future

The grandfather of Deep Ecology teaches us how to move
from a human-centered view of the world to one focused on
the earth and all its inhabitants.
0-609-80499-5 · *Softcover*

Cynthia Bourgeault
LOVE IS STRONGER THAN DEATH
The Mystical Union of Two Souls

Both the story of the incandescent love between two hermits
and a guidebook for those called to this path of soulwork.
0-609-60473-2 · *Hardcover*

Madeline Bruser
THE ART OF PRACTICING
Making Music from the Heart

A classic work on how to practice music that combines
meditative principles with information on body mechanics
and medicine.

0-609-80177-5 • *Softcover*

Thomas Byrom (Trans.)
THE DHAMMAPADA
The Sayings of the Buddha

The first book in a series of small spiritual classics
entitled Sacred Teachings.

0-609-60888-6 • *Hardcover*

Marc David
NOURISHING WISDOM
*A Mind/Body Approach to Nutrition
and Well-Being*

A book that advocates awareness in eating.

0-517-88129-2 • *Softcover*

Joan Furman, M.S.N., R.N., and David McNabb
THE DYING TIME
Practical Wisdom for the Dying and Their Caregivers

A comprehensive guide, filled with physical, emotional,
and spiritual advice.

0-609-80003-5 • *Softcover*

Bernard Glassman
BEARING WITNESS
A Zen Master's Lessons in Making Peace

How Glassman started the Zen Peacemaker Order and what
each of us can do to make peace in our hearts and in the world.
0-609-60061-3 · *Hardcover* / 0-609-80391-3 · *Softcover*

Bernard Glassman and Rick Fields
INSTRUCTIONS TO THE COOK
A Zen Master's Lessons in Living a Life That Matters

A distillation of Zen wisdom that can be used equally well as a
manual on business or spiritual practice, cooking or life.
0-517-88829-7 · *Softcover*

Niles Elliot Goldstein
GOD AT THE EDGE
*Searching for the Divine in Uncomfortable
and Unexpected Places*

A book about adventure, raw experience, and facing
inner demons.
0-609-60499-6 · *Hardcover* / 0-609-80488-X · *Softcover*

Greg Johanson and Ron Kurtz
GRACE UNFOLDING
Psychotherapy in the Spirit of the Tao-te ching

The interaction of client and therapist illuminated through the
gentle power and wisdom of Lao Tsu's ancient classic.
0-517-88130-6 · *Softcover*

Selected by Marcia and Jack Kelly

ONE HUNDRED GRACES

Mealtime Blessings

A collection of graces from many traditions, inscribed
in calligraphy reminiscent of the manuscripts of
medieval Europe.

0-609-80093-0 · *Softcover*

Jack and Marcia Kelly

SANCTUARIES

*A Guide to Lodgings in Monasteries, Abbeys,
and Retreats of the United States*

For those in search of renewal and a little peace;
described by the *New York Times* as "the *Michelin Guide*
of the retreat set."

0-517-88517-4 · *Softcover*

Lorraine Kisly, ed.

ORDINARY GRACES

Christian Teachings on the Interior Life

An essential collection of the deepest spiritual, religious, and
psychological teachings of Christianity.

0-609-60674-3 · *Hardcover* / 0-609-80618-1 · *Softcover*

Barbara Lachman

THE JOURNAL OF HILDEGARD OF BINGEN

A year in the life of the twelfth-century German saint—
the diary she never had the time to write herself.

0-517-88390-2 · *Softcover*

Stephen Levine
A YEAR TO LIVE
How to Live This Year As If It Were Your Last

Using the consciousness of our mortality to enter into a new and
vibrant relationship with life.

0-609-80194-5 • *Softcover*

Helen M. Luke
OLD AGE
Journey into Simplicity

A classic text on how to age wisely by one of the
great Jungian analysts of our time.

0-609-80590-8 • *Softcover*

Helen M. Luke
SUCH STUFF AS DREAMS ARE MADE ON
The Autobiography and Journals of Helen M. Luke

A memoir, 140 pages culled from the 54 volumes of her
journals, and 45 black-and-white photos—the summation
of her life and work.

0-609-80589-4 • *Softcover*

Marcia Prager
THE PATH OF BLESSING
Experiencing the Energy and Abundance of the Divine

How to use the traditional Jewish practice of calling down a
blessing on each action as a profound path of spiritual growth.

0-517-70363-7 • *Hardcover* / 0-609-80393-X • *Softcover*

Saki Santorelli
HEAL THY SELF
Lessons on Mindfulness in Medicine

An invitation to patients and health care professionals
to bring mindfulness into the crucible of the
healing relationship.
0-609-60385-X · *Hardcover* / 0-609-80504-5 · *Softcover*

Rabbi Rami M. Shapiro
MINYAN
Ten Principles for Living a Life of Integrity

A primer for those interested to know what Judaism has
to offer the spiritually hungry.
0-609-80055-8 · *Softcover*

Rabbi Rami M. Shapiro
WISDOM OF THE JEWISH SAGES
A Modern Reading of Pirke Avot

A third-century treasury of maxims on justice, integrity, and
virtue—Judaism's principal ethical scripture.
0-517-79966-9 · *Hardcover*

Jean Smith
THE BEGINNER'S GUIDE TO ZEN BUDDHISM

A comprehensive and easily accessible introduction that
assumes no prior knowledge of Zen Buddhism.
0-609-80466-9 · *Softcover*